THIS IS ME! 2022

AMAZING WORDS

Edited By Byron Tobolik

First published in Great Britain in 2022 by:

Young Writers Est. 1991

Young Writers
Remus House
Coltsfoot Drive
Peterborough
PE2 9BF
Telephone: 01733 890066
Website: www.youngwriters.co.uk

Printed and bound in the UK by BookPrintingUK
Website: www.bookprintinguk.com
YB0521D

FOREWORD

*For Young Writers' latest competition This Is Me,
we asked primary school pupils to look inside
themselves, to think about what makes them unique,
and then write a poem about it! They rose to the
challenge magnificently and the result is this fantastic
collection of poems in a variety of poetic styles.*

*Here at Young Writers our aim is to encourage creativity
in children and to inspire a love of the written word, so
it's great to get such an amazing response, with some
absolutely fantastic poems. It's important for children to
focus on and celebrate themselves and this competition
allowed them to write freely and honestly, celebrating
what makes them great, expressing their hopes and
fears, or simply writing about their favourite things.
This Is Me gave them the power of words. The result
is a collection of inspirational and moving poems that
also showcase their creativity and writing ability.*

*I'd like to congratulate all the young poets
in this anthology, I hope this inspires them
to continue with their creative writing.*

CONTENTS

Fitrah Southampton Islamic Primary School, Southampton

Haroon Rahimi	60

Larkholme Primary School, Fleetwood

Grace Boyle (7)	61

Myddelton College, Denbigh

Sovay Hall (11)	62

Nishkam Primary School, Wolverhampton

Charan Dadrah	64

Orchard Vale Primary School, Whiddon Valley

Natalie (11)	65
Kaito Roseveare (11)	66
Chloe-Rose Squire (11)	67
Mya Turl (11)	68
Morganna Howell (11)	69
George Ellis (11)	70
Ava Barrow (11)	72
Naima Hawes (11)	73
Michael Holland-Borley (11)	74
William Rogers (10)	75
Florence Hill (11)	76
Logan Kenwood (11)	77
Sophie Glover (11)	78
Ria Laird (11)	79
Harrison Vessey (11)	80
Phineas Hughes (11)	81
Ethan Thorne (11)	82
Joseph Keeble (11)	83
Olivia Popps (11)	84
Oliver Thorne (11)	85

Roecliffe CE Primary School, Roecliffe

Tempi Singhateh	86
Lucy G (9)	88
William Bennett (8)	90
Isla C (8)	91
Milosz Smentek (9)	92
George R	93
Edward Wright (9)	94
Isabella Campbell (8)	95
Georgina L	96
Ida P (9)	97

St Joseph's Catholic Primary School, Deptford

Benita Bagnall (9)	98
Chiamaka Onwochei (9)	99
Betsy Ebenuwa (8)	100
Destiny Onyewachi (9)	102
Enoch Akinsomisoye (9)	103
Chantelle Osei (9)	104
Maya Hamdoun (9)	105
Patricia Krotka (9)	106
Prince Armah Erzoah (8)	107
Elisha Brainard (9)	108
Adanna Nnani (9)	109
Christian Kelly (9)	110

St Mary's RC Primary School, Wimbledon

Angus Campbell (11)	111
Troy Edwards (11)	112
Julia Ornowska (11)	114
Francesca Brooks (10)	116
Adriana Ramos (11)	118
Gabriella Wilson (10)	120
Hailey Chan (11)	122
Nikol Pilichowska (11)	124
Amelia Ciecka (11)	126
Ellie Narainsamy Mouriz (11)	128
Elano Jorge (11)	130

Hugo Barra (11)	132
Georgia Kelly (11)	134
Helen Golus (11)	136
Iliana Turbin (11)	138
Isabel Bonney (11)	140
Sophii Skrzynska (11)	141
Amelia Kelly (11)	142
Carolina Pontes Fernandes (11)	143
Leo Farag (11)	144
Martina Cardenas (11)	145
Alexandra El Khoury (11)	146
Marko Dobrovolskyi (11)	148
Aiden Farrugia (11)	149
Aëlis Joalland (11)	150
Georgia Bate (11)	152
Grace Castelli (10)	153
Amelia Maria Nyack (11)	154
Madalena Orvalho (11)	155
Tabitha Keefe (8)	156
Lukasz Zelazowski (11)	157
Georgie Brooks (9)	158
Maya Sputo (8)	159
Helena Bourbon (9)	160
Arianna Vallejo de Lange (11)	161
Laura Scripps (11)	162
Capucine Tanqueray (11)	163
Stefano La Rosa (11)	164
Thomas Cruz (11)	165
Noah Simpson (11)	166

Sundridge & Brasted CE (VC) Primary School, Sundridge

Mia Wallis-Figa (10)	167
Charlie Hawley (11)	168
Nate De Bono (11)	169
Amelia Newlands (9)	170
Willow Sawkins (9)	171

Willington Prep School, Wimbledon

Ram Bhalla Singh (9)	172
James Douglas (8)	173

Perry Davis (8)	174
Kieran Bourne (10)	175
Nathan Whooley (8)	176
William Booth (10)	177

Woodbridge Park Education Service, Isleworth

Kenzie Lowe (11)	178

THE POEMS

This Is Who I Am

R arely, I keep quiet.
O bedient? I am.
N oticeable? I think I am.
N eighbourly? They think I am.
I rritated? Maybe.
E nthusiastic? Somewhere around that.

J olly? I think, yes.
A wesome? I'm not so sure.
C alm? I don't think so.
K ind? That is hard to find.

I am Ronnie-Jack.
This is me!

Ronnie-Jack Jones (11)
Caslon Primary School, Halesowen

What It Really Is

"Here are some rainbow crayons," said Sir.
Okay, before I start, I must line up the crayons.
But all the points have to be at the same end.
Now they aren't all in line!
But then it has to be in rainbow order.
Okay, let's start drawing...
"End of lesson!"

Okay, I'm at Mia's!
Knock, knock.
If I don't knock three times, I will... mmm, faint.
Knock, knock, knock.
Okay, four because it has to be even.
Knock, knock, knock, knock.
But if not six times, something will happen to my family.
Knock, knock, knock, knock, knock, knock.
"Okay, I'm here, stop knocking!" shouted Mia.

"Mum, please can we get an extension?" I asked.
"Why?"

"Because the house isn't symmetrical," I replied.
"No!" Mum shouted angrily.

Why am I like this?
Guess the disorder...

Alicia Jane Spence (11)

Caslon Primary School, Halesowen

Are You?

Are you brave?
I wouldn't say so.
Are you tall?
No, not really.
Are you a billionaire?
Who do you think I am, Elon Musk?
Are you famous?
I wish!
Are you an adult?
Haha, no!
Are you in high school?
Soon...
Hmm, who are you then?
I'm me and I wouldn't change it for the world.

Bella-Rose Young (11)
Caslon Primary School, Halesowen

I Am Someone Who...

I am someone who likes doing things quickly.
I am someone who doesn't like losing or I will get angry.
I am someone who always gets 39 marks in maths.
I am someone who likes to be happy.
I am someone who is kind to my brother.
I am someone who always gets hit by a ball.
This is me.

Lu Chun Yin Lu (11)
Caslon Primary School, Halesowen

It's Good To Be Me

I wanted to study acupuncture,
But my mum said there was no point.
I got a job as a zookeeper,
But they kept on saying that I was monkeying around.
I wanted to be an astronaut,
But there wasn't that much space.
But really, all I want in the world...
Is to be me.

Dominic Lane (11)
Caslon Primary School, Halesowen

My Sister, Leah Evans!

L oving to animals and family
E xcellent dancer
A wesome singer
H ilarious at jokes

E verything is right
V alues love
A ctive at karate
N ice to family and friends
S mart at maths.

Lexi Grainger (10)
Caslon Primary School, Halesowen

Who Am I?

I am someone who likes to cook,
I am someone who likes dogs,
I am someone who crashes into a tree,
I am someone who loves their dad,
I am someone who likes the whole world,
I am someone who is addicted to their phone,
I am me.

Hannah Louise Victoria Sprintall (10)

Caslon Primary School, Halesowen

Unstoppable Me!

Let me take this opportunity to introduce you to
my life,
For almost a decade, I have been alive,
I have been on a roller coaster of pleasure and
grief,
Nothing will alter my relief.

I see myself touch the sky,
Looking up and feeling so high,
I aspire to become a diligent doctor,
I aspire to become a famous actor.

My love is attached to nature,
The lush green grass and colourful blossoms,
The adorable playful animals,
The magnificent forests of tall trees.

I wonder what I'm yet to learn about me,
Having things that even we don't see!
I'm not affected by the negative you say to me,
I am about as perfect as I can be,
I'm always beaming and buzzing like a bee,
And that is all I can say about me!

Aisha Desai (10)
Cleveland Road Primary School, Ilford

Who Am I?

My friends and everyone say I'm great,
My little brothers say I'm not,
My parents say I'm the best.
Me? I don't think so.
Am I loyal? Yes.
I support and help whoever needs it,
Especially my brothers and friends, of course.
Do I care? Yes.
If someone has a nasty injury, I help them up,
Even if I don't know them, just in case they get
stuck.
Skilful? Maybe.
I have writing skills, listening skills,
My friends say I'm skilled in sports, we may also
add that.
Am I eco-friendly? Sure...?
I help the environment as often as I can,
I may not be the eco-warrior in my class but it
really doesn't matter.
Am I serious? A little.
Just so my team can do their best and try to win,
But winning isn't everything, it's just fun you need.

I might be nice or I might not,
I'm not too good or too bad...
You know what?
I think I'm perfect just the way I am.

Nawaal Khan

Cleveland Road Primary School, Ilford

All About Me

If you ask who am I,
You will see straight from the eye,
I am me, just me,
But not the same as many.

I know my future is not the same,
Why am I different by the name?
I'm just saying that I'm not you,
If we were the same, then who is who?

Maybe I'm brave, maybe I'm not,
But I'm just one from that big lot,
I'm daring, I'm fast,
When learning, I'm never last.

There are many things that I don't know,
But I know I love my family, I love my home,
When you look in my eye, maybe you're glad,
But sometimes you can be depressed or sad.

If you ask who am I,
You will see straight from the eye,

I am me, just me,
But not the same as many.

Pranshi Rathod (9)
Cleveland Road Primary School, Ilford

This Is Me

I like football,
This is me.
I like running as fast as the wind,
This is me.
I like hope,
This is me.
I like writing like Charlotte with her webs,
This is me.
I like playing,
This is me.
I like to be a role model,
This is me.
I like drawing,
This is me.
I like helping children and people that are poor,
This is me.
I like to be equal,
This is me.
I like planting more and more,
This is me.

I like saving paper,
This is me.
I like changing the climate, the seas and stopping trees from being cut down,
This is me.
I like shining like the sun,
This is me.

Alina

Cleveland Road Primary School, Ilford

This Is Me

My name is Hisham,
I am friendly and kind,
My name means generous.

So I shall be,
I like playing games,
I make mistakes, so?
Everybody does.

I have two brothers,
One annoying and one naughty,
But I still love them.

I am as fast as a cheetah,
As brave as a lion.

Sometimes I'm happy,
Sometimes I'm angry,
Sometimes I'm strong.

Sometimes I'm weak,
Sometimes I'm right,
Sometimes I'm wrong.

But still, I love myself,
And will try to improve as well.

Muhhamad Hisham Shakir (9)

Cleveland Road Primary School, Ilford

Spider-Man, Spider-Man

Spider-Man, Spider-Man,
We all love you, Spider-Man.
Everyone dreams about Spider-Man,
Spider-Man is powerful,
He can solve any problem,
He has superpowers.
"I love Spider-Man, I am a Spider-Boy!"
"He is nice, Spider-Man."
"He is kind, Spider-Man."
Spider-Man, please come to London,
Show me your web wires,
Lend me some webs, Spider-Man,
You are very helpful, Spider-Man.
"Sharing is caring, Spider-Man."
"Share your powers, Spider-Man."
We love you, Spider-Man.

Aryan Yousaf (7)
Cleveland Road Primary School, Ilford

I Am Me And Proud

I am a person like everyone else

Am I proud of it?
Me, only me, has special abilities

Me and I am special
Every day, I have fun playing with my friends

And writing a bunch of stories
Never have I not been sad
Do I want to change?

I know I'm special though
Many people tell me

Proud, proud of me
Really? Yes, I think so
Over my dead body, will anyone make fun of me
Underneath, I'm still proud of who I'm meant to be
Do I care? Yes and I'm proud of me.

Subaita Islam (10)
Cleveland Road Primary School, Ilford

Why Me?

I entered the world on 4th December 2014,
To give the biggest gift to my queen.

I am charming and caring,
And sometimes very daring.
I love being me,
But stupid enough to be stung by a bee.
Being friendly and loud is my gift,
But don't annoy me, I can pull up a fist.
You have to be as cold as ice,
To be a doctor in disguise.
I will achieve and fulfil my dream,
By working with an amazing team.
Being this fabulous is hard work,
Having great skills and amazing artwork.

Amelia Hussain (7)
Cleveland Road Primary School, Ilford

Soul

As a breath of winter air seems just like smoke,
I'm a secret no one dares to know,
Like a broken vase,
The heart can explain love no further,
You must look at yourself,
In yourself,
In a place of people with big ideas,
Even I am not the same,
Even I cannot find myself in the biggest crowd,
In a world full of mayhem, drama and sorrow,
Love, pain and kindness,
It is hard to see,
The world is strange but balanced,
Like a soul,
That soul is me,
Got your answer?

Tanya Kaur
Cleveland Road Primary School, Ilford

All About Me

I am energetic, full of joy,
I like to be kind and caring,
People say I'm an adventurous boy,
Life is short, let's enjoy,
Black and white are my favourite colours,
Sometimes I am angry like a storm,
All I want is to be cheered by others,
Kindness makes me reform,
She is as sweet as honey,
A million apples in the tree,
She says I am her bunny,
Up in the sky, I want to go free,
To check all the planets,
An astronaut I want to be.

Abbas Hussain (6)
Cleveland Road Primary School, Ilford

This Is Me

This is me as bright as the sun,
Shining high in the sky.

This is me, creative like an artist,
Full of bright ideas and colours.
This is me.

This is me as colourful as a rainbow,
Shining and shimmering in the rain.

This is me as big as the ocean,
This is me making the world more peaceful.

This is me making a change,
This is me saving the plants,
This is me making the world a better place.

Noureen
Cleveland Road Primary School, Ilford

This Is Me!

This is me,
Living free,
At times, I want,
To be by myself,
To be happy,
I exchange smiles,
With friends,
With family.

I like life,
I like me,
I want to be,
A person in life,
Who spares time,
We will end crime,
We live happily,
We stay happy,
We are happy.

I am a girl,
A quiet, normal girl,

I will walk through nightmares,
I will walk through dreams,
This is me!

Umaiza
Cleveland Road Primary School, Ilford

Young Writers Est. 1991

My Poetic Self

Eshaal is my name which is,
The most fragrant in Heaven,
I am as fresh as a cool breeze in the summer,
As colourful as a rainbow after the rain,
As kind as a mother's love,
As cute as a baby,
As soft as a teddy bear,
As warm-hearted as a sunbeam,
Caring like an angel,
A doctor is what I want to become,
To help other people,
To love and spread love,
I want to make them proud,
My siblings, Mommy and Dad.

Eshaal Saqib (7)
Cleveland Road Primary School, Ilford

What Do I See?

What do I see when I look in the mirror?
Always up to mischief but never wanting to be blamed,
It wasn't me! It wasn't me! I've been framed.

Sharing the kindness, making people smile,
Always telling jokes and going the extra mile.

What do I see when I look in the mirror?
A happy person full of laughter,
An artist, an actor, a comedy creator.

That's what I see when I look in the mirror.

Mishal Akram (10)
Cleveland Road Primary School, Ilford

This Is Me

Today is my day,
I am going to find a way,
This is me.
I am the wind on a warm morning,
Listening to the roaring cars as they sing.
I know it is not right, so I say...
Stop the pollution,
Stop the cars, find a way,
Stop the world from dying,
Today!
This is our world for ever and ever,
We can't live on Mars or Jupiter,
Planet Earth is our home,
Help the world with me.
This is me!

Sofia Awan (9)
Cleveland Road Primary School, Ilford

About Me

My name is Amani,
Let me tell you about me,
I am as soft as jelly,
Who wouldn't want to be so smelly?
I'd rather be outside when it's sunny,
So I can be a shiny bunny,
People think I am cool,
Well, let me tell you that's true,
I believe there's a tree that grows money,
Like a growing fruit,
I wish we could find it, but we can't.

Amani (7)
Cleveland Road Primary School, Ilford

This Is Me!

I'm about as certain as I can be,
That all of us, to some degree,
Have things that even we can't see,
I wonder what I'm yet to learn about me?
I know I am not the person I will be tomorrow,
Nor the me from the past,
Shaped by other days that followed,
I'm here in my moment, that's all I can be,
And that's all I can say about me.

Nukhba Gillani (9)
Cleveland Road Primary School, Ilford

I Am Me

I am me,
I love Lego,
It builds anything,
Vroom, vroom! goes the car.

I am me,
I like games,
Games fuel my creativity,
Like petrol filling a car.

I am me,
I love maths,
It's like a puzzle,
The answer: hidden.

I am me,
I am special,
I am unique,
I am one of a kind.

Muhammad Ullah (10)
Cleveland Road Primary School, Ilford

Inside Abrish

Inside me is a friendly unicorn,
Who plays with friends all day,
Inside me is an old unicorn,
Who lays in bed till sunrise,
Inside me is a clean unicorn,
Who loves showers,
Inside me is a naughty unicorn,
Who plays tricks on everyone,
Inside me is a funny unicorn,
When I tell a joke, I can't stop laughing.

Abrish Sikander (6)
Cleveland Road Primary School, Ilford

This Is Me

T oday, I will pray,

H elp older people,

I will enjoy everything,

S o don't throw trash in the sea,

I f you forget, put it in the bin,

S ee people and copy good things,

M ake everyone happy and not sad,

E njoy being you, this is me, I do!

Hana Maryam Akram (8)

Cleveland Road Primary School, Ilford

Definition Of Vikram

This is me, I am Vikram,
I am as happy as a lark,
When I go to the park,
I have always dreamt of being an astronaut,
I am also into robots,
I go to sleep and switch off the light,
As the moon goes up in the night,
My family are like a hive of bees,
When I am the happiest person I can be.

Vikram Sai Arun (6)
Cleveland Road Primary School, Ilford

This Is Me

I will be there for you whenever,
If it rains, you can come under my umbrella,
As I walk down the sadness, I make flowers bloom,
But when I'm angry, they go *boom!*
And I like to stay in my room,
Although I'm crazy, I do get lazy,
I like to write and explore new worlds.

Kashmala Gul (10)
Cleveland Road Primary School, Ilford

Raza

My heart leaps up when I behold,
A rainbow in the sky,
So it was when my life began,
So it is now I am a man,
So be it when I shall grow old,
Or let me die!
The child is the father of the man,
And I could wish my days to be,
Bound each to each
By natural piety.

Raza (9)
Cleveland Road Primary School, Ilford

This Is Me

I'm ambitious, charming as well,
I like to play everything, that makes me fun,
Sun, rain, clouds and wind are cheerful,
With friends in mind, I go to play,
We are beautiful, hard-working and good,
Whenever I need help, I'm always loving,
That's my style.

Razvan George Musca (7)
Cleveland Road Primary School, Ilford

My Dreams And Me

I am helpful,
I am kind,
I am funny,
I am cheeky.

I kick a football,
I shoot a basketball,
I surf a king ball,
I dodge a dodgeball.

I want to fly a plane,
Even if it rains,
I better not go in the drain,
Let's play again.

Uzair Kashif (9)
Cleveland Road Primary School, Ilford

Cosy Kangaroo

I am a cosy kangaroo,
I want to be a police officer in a year or two.
Sitting on Tower Bridge,
Eating goat's cheese.
Playing with Abrish in the park,
Until it gets dark.
Reading books, drinking milk, eating a banana,
That is wow, oh, la, la!

Maahira Mandiwal (7)
Cleveland Road Primary School, Ilford

This Is Me

I like to draw cartoon characters,
My favourite character is Darwin,
He is from my favourite show,
Sometimes I do puzzles if I'm bored,
I like drinking cherryade when I am thirsty,
My favourite food is pasta,
And I eat it sometimes for dinner.

Iqra Jhumka (7)
Cleveland Road Primary School, Ilford

Annoying Me

I am happy like a shooting star,
I know I am annoying but I am the best,
I care about others and me!
I love being myself,
Because it makes me smile!
I am grateful for everything in the world.
I am the one and only prankster.

Suwarsha Suman (10)
Cleveland Road Primary School, Ilford

This Is Me

T rusting
H elping
I nside
S inging

I nside
S haring

M oving
E njoying.

I enjoy helping my mum clean the garden.

Hafsa Sharjeel (8)
Cleveland Road Primary School, Ilford

This Is All About Me

I am shy,
I am very quiet,
I love painting and colouring,
And I also love gardening.

I like being organised,
My favourite colour is blue,
So this is me,
But what about you?

Umm-l-Habiba Sethi (10)
Cleveland Road Primary School, Ilford

About Me

As the wind goes,
I never give up,
I run as fast as I can,
I won a medal for sports day,
I am as kind as a flower,
I am as helpful as a plant.

Yuna Khan (10)
Cleveland Road Primary School, Ilford

The Recipe That Makes Me!

One litre of kindness,
Two cups of tenderness,
One spoon of forgiveness,
One pinch of arguments,
And that makes me!

Maryam Chowdhury (7)
Cleveland Road Primary School, Ilford

Friendship

Roses are red, violets are blue,
My name is Jannat and I love you.
Will you be my friend?
And I will play with you too.

Jannat
Cleveland Road Primary School, Ilford

Mahir The Footballer

I am a strong footballer,
I am a nice footballer,
I have lots of friends,
I am calm,
I love movies.

Mohammed Mahir Akhtar (6)

Cleveland Road Primary School, Ilford

Me!

I love rabbits and I have habits,
I am fast and I am slow,
Let's have a race and I'll watch you go!
I have a sister and I have a brother,
I have a dad and I have a mother.
If you see me on the street,
I will wave and give you a treat.
I like books and I love new looks,
I want to learn about space,
And I like to run and pick up the pace!
And of course, that's wonderful me,
Filled with glorious me,
So different and filled with glee!

Keira Meehan (8)
Colman Junior School, Norwich

My Hat

I am a girl much like the rest,
But I have a hat that is the best.

To school or to bed, I don't care,
I wear my hat everywhere.

It comes from Finland, it has a name,
There is no hat that is quite the same.

Finny, it is called,
And without it, I feel quite bald.

Red swirls on white, it is quite a sight.
If you could see, I'm sure you'd agree.

Whatever the weather, rain or storm,
This hat keeps me warm.

Sarah Valente (8)
Colman Junior School, Norwich

This Is Me!

I am loved by my family,
I am in love with glitter and pandas.
Here is a recipe for me:
A sprinkle of a smile into the jar.
Okay, in go the cupcakes and the sweets go in too.
They all go *plop, plop, plop.*
What's next on the list?
Well, a gerbil and it's almost done.
A phone, *plop.* A TV, *plop.* A tablet, *plop.*

Natalia Brown (8)
Colman Junior School, Norwich

The Buzzing Bee

I'm a bee buzzing in a tree,
And I don't like the sea,
Because I'm a bee flying in the sky,
I'm a bee soaring here and there,
Because I'm a bee,
I live in a tree,
And everyone I know is a bee,
Because I'm a bee.

Finbar Packer (8)
Colman Junior School, Norwich

This Is Me!

I have a dream to be a footballer.
The last match we played, we won 5-3.
I support Liverpool;
I have been to the stadium on a tour.
It was fun,
I saw the big sun,
I got some clothes, it was fun.
I dream of playing in that stadium.

Henry Shakespeare (7)

Colman Junior School, Norwich

My Name Is Sidney

S idney, that's me

I like scooting

D oughnuts, I love them

N aughty, that's not me

E ating, I absolutely love it

Y ippee! My name is Sid.

Sidney Barton (7)

Colman Junior School, Norwich

Some Days

Some days we are happy,
Some days we are sad,
Some days everything is fun,
Some days it's all a bore.

But each day without exception,
I love you more and more.

Laila Boudjelal (7)
Colman Junior School, Norwich

This Is Me!

A kennings poem

Cat lover,
Minecraft lover,
Pink hater,
Bike rider,
Roblox liker,
Blue looker,
Kind helper,
Fidget lover,
Book lover,
Dog lover,
Stitch lover,
Who am I?
I am me.

Cyannah Lovett (8)
Colman Junior School, Norwich

This Is Me!

A kennings poem

Prune hater,
Panda lover,
Rabbit owner,
Pink liker,
Quick runner,
Fun player,
Good drawer,
Book writer!

Lydia Harris (7)
Colman Junior School, Norwich

This Is Me!

A kennings poem

Bunny lover,
Ice cream licker,
Spider hater,
Year 3 student,
Teddy bear lover,
Minecraft player.

Alice Moore (8)
Colman Junior School, Norwich

Pru, It Is Me

P retty

R uby

U nique.

Pru Knott (7)

Colman Junior School, Norwich

My Life, My Story

Hello, my name is Orla,
I have a dog, I have a cat,
But most of all, I want a rat.
I like yellow, I like purple,
And my friend has a turtle.
I am in Gryffindor,
I have a white door leading to my bedroom,
Oh, what a fuss.
I like football,
I'm not so good at netball,
And my neighbour's called Paul.
I'm a writer, I'm a reader,
And I am a vast believer.
I have two sisters,
One is ginger, one is brown.
I have ginger hair and blue eyes,
Oh, how I feel alive.
I am Orla.

Orla Brunstrom (9)
Downs Junior School, Brighton

This Is Me

H aroon is my name
A crobats are lame, football is my game
R onaldo is the best footballer
O range is my favourite fruit
O ldest brother to my siblings
N eed to take care of them all

R esourcefully artistic
A ccommodating to all
H elpful all around
I ncredibly polite
M astering mathematics
I s what my teachers say.

Haroon Rahimi
Fitrah Southampton Islamic Primary School, Southampton

Great Grace

My name is Grace and I'm seven (nearly eight),
I like doing English - I am great!
My favourite colour is shiny sunset yellow,
I like it when the sun says hello!
My gramps makes the best green, healthy soup,
It's spicy and yummy and not like gloop!
I play with my sisters; we make slime,
When I go to the park, I like to climb.
When I'm older, I want to teach in a beautiful, calm school,
I think this will be super cool!
My name's Grace and I'm nearly eight,
I might be tiny but I am great!

Grace Boyle (7)

Larkholme Primary School, Fleetwood

City Of Eyes

Light, flowing eyes, slowly engulfed by dark,
mysterious circles,
Soft, pink lips below dark, patterned glasses,
Thin, blonde hair preferring to be free and let
loose,
Dented in my cheeks, dimples appear as the
corners of my mouth lift,
Why do I look like this?

Ombré of blues reflected in my pupils, mask
rubbing against my face,
The outline of dark, 2D mountains pressed against
the sky,
The silenced buzz of the vehicle driving on the
concrete,
Talking and shouting is heard, making me think,
Why do I have to take this bus?

Wondering, thinking, watching,
Watching the world we live in and the lives we
have,
Thinking about how blessed I am to be here,

Wondering about everyone's lives and what it must be like,
Will I ever be in someone else's eyes?

Sovay Hall (11)

Myddelton College, Denbigh

The River

The river's an angel,
Soft and gentle,
It dances in the striking sunlight,
And glistens in the mystic moonlight,
The river's a mirror,
It shimmers and shines,
It reflects the world's beauty,
Until the river changes its mind,
It gives a loud roar,
Making its way to the shore,
The river's a sinister snake,
Which twists and turns,
It slithers through the land,
And there's no hope of return,
The river's a monster,
Hungry and wild,
It swallows up trees,
And gives shakes to the knees,
Without saying sorry or please,
After taking its victory,
It all becomes history.

Charan Dadrah
Nishkam Primary School, Wolverhampton

Everything You Need To Know About Natalie Phillips

N   is for Natalie and this poem is about me

A   is for amazing and that is one of the things I am

T   is for terrific and that sounds cool

A   is for awesome and I just don't know

L   is for lovely and that is what I am

I   is for incredible and that is another thing I am

E   is for excellent and I do excellent work

P   is for posh, well, I guess I am fancy

H   is for happy and I am most of the time

I   is for indescribable since I can't think of anything that starts with I

L   is for loyal and I am in every way

L   is for loving and I do that 24/7

I   is for imaginary and that is something I can do

P   is for perfect and I am in every way

S   is for superstar because I am one, I guess.

Natalie (11)

Orchard Vale Primary School, Whiddon Valley

All About Me

K aito is my name
A nd my aim:
I will try new things every day
T ravelling the beauties of this world and eating healthy every day
O r maybe I can just stay

R oseveare is my last name
O pportunities are standing for me
S ome might even be my future degree
E ager every day to have fun after school
V aluable moments I am living through
E ager to play out with friends
A pples are my favourite fruit, and that's true
R ain is a common occurrence down here, but when we get sun it's always good
E ven when I'm in a bad mood.

Kaito Roseveare (11)
Orchard Vale Primary School, Whiddon Valley

This Is Me!

My heart is racing as the curtains open,
The show begins, the audience: frozen,
As the music starts, I glide on stage,
Like a character from a book, I leap off the page.

Elegantly I float, expressing my emotion,
I turn and I stretch and I move like the ocean.
As I spring rapidly into the air,
Extending my arms, the audience glare.

The atmosphere changes as the music intensifies,
I look into the audience and gaze deep into their
eyes,
The cheering erupts with a deafening roar,
Just as I land gracefully upon the floor.

When the lights become low,
I know that's the end of the show...

Chloe-Rose Squire (11)
Orchard Vale Primary School, Whiddon Valley

I Am Mya

I am Mya,
I have my opinions and points of view,
I am independent and strong,
I believe what I think is true,
With a strong sense of what's right and what's wrong,
But that never comes out.

I am Mya,
I am sensitive and shy,
I am confident on the inside,
I know I don't need to cry,
And I know I don't need to hide,
But that never comes out.

I am Mya,
I am powerful and great,
But no one seems to know,
Because at the moment, I am small and lightweight,
But soon, everyone will see me glow,
Someday, this will all come out.

Mya Turl (11)
Orchard Vale Primary School, Whiddon Valley

This Is Me

My name is Morganna and this describes me,
I am as crazy as can be.

This is who I am!

So I'm crazy and sometimes I act royal,
Although I am not only crazy but loyal.

This is who I am!

I love sharing,
So I guess that makes me caring.

This is who I am!

Resilient I am, no, I don't give up,
Someday I'd love to have a little pup.

This is who I am!

If only you knew how animal-loving I am,
However, I do love jam.

This is who I am, don't be afraid to be you!

Morganna Howell (11)
Orchard Vale Primary School, Whiddon Valley

This Is Me

G reat
E xcellent story writer
O bservant
R esilient
G reat at English
E nergetic

M ovie lover
A ctually a chill person
R eally funny
K ind (sometimes)

T houghtful
H appy
O verthinker
M akes Lego
A dventurous
S tar Wars is awesome

E llis
L ikes to ride scooters and bikes
L oves family
I like to write
S cooters are cool.

George Ellis (11)
Orchard Vale Primary School, Whiddon Valley

This Is Me

A spoonful of sweetness,
A dollop of humour,
A jar of delicate intelligence,
A pool of creativity,
Although all these things make up me,
Mostly because my mind is full of activity!
Friends with hope,
Even when it's hard to cope,
Love for family and friends,
I am grateful for them all,
Though with all my chatter, it's quite a haul,
I'm full of ideas,
So put some of that in too,
Now stir it up into a delightful stew,
Or perhaps stir something new?

Ava Barrow (11)
Orchard Vale Primary School, Whiddon Valley

All About Me

N eymar Jr is my nickname

A wesome family and friends surrounding me

I love all sports but football is where my passion is

M aking creative things with my mum for fun

A nd this is me!

H aving fun with my friends

A nd hoping to play for Liverpool FC when I'm older

W hen playing football, I think of nothing else

E specially when I'm on the pitch!

S o this is me.

Naima Hawes (11)

Orchard Vale Primary School, Whiddon Valley

All About Me!

Hi, my name is Michael,
I like to cycle.

I do parkour,
What I adore:

Martial arts,
And I like riding in Tesco shopping carts!

I don't like maths,
I like hot baths.

I'm a massive fan of Cobra Kai,
If a new season doesn't come out soon, I'm gonna
die!

Michael Holland-Borley (11)
Orchard Vale Primary School, Whiddon Valley

This Is Me

My name is William Rogers, I'm a little bit loud,
To be a pupil at Orchard Vale, I am very proud,
I enjoy all my lessons and am eager to learn more,
All the teachers at school are really top drawer,
I also love sports,
And always in shorts,
My poem is done,
So is my fun.

William Rogers (10)

Orchard Vale Primary School, Whiddon Valley

This Is Me

F orever chatting
L oving life
O bviously tall
R eliable footballer
E ntertainingly different
N ever negative, always positive
C aring to friends and family
E xcellent imagination, always dreaming.

Florence Hill (11)

Orchard Vale Primary School, Whiddon Valley

The Dark Side Of Me

I look happy on the outside but the inside is
burning,
I don't feel pain but inside it's burning,
When I look down, I'm not hiding,
The monster inside me is fighting and fighting,
But I will win because my friends will cheer me up.

Logan Kenwood (11)

Orchard Vale Primary School, Whiddon Valley

This Is Me

S hy and nervous
O bservant and alert
P olite and respectful
H appy and joyful
I maginative and creative
E mpathetic and compassionate.

Sophie Glover (11)
Orchard Vale Primary School, Whiddon Valley

Ria

R esilient

I maginative

A mazing at games and sports

L ucky

A ctive

I ncognito

R esourceful

D istinctive.

Ria Laird (11)

Orchard Vale Primary School, Whiddon Valley

All About Me!

H appy
A dventurous
R idiculous
R idiculous
I ntelligent
S ucceeding
O verly good at games
N ever gives up.

Harrison Vessey (11)

Orchard Vale Primary School, Whiddon Valley

This Is Me!

P assionate

H appy

I ntent

N oble

E nlightened

A wesome

S o happy to be me! I love myself, my family and my friends.

Phineas Hughes (11)

Orchard Vale Primary School, Whiddon Valley

This Is Me

There was a young lad called Ethan,
He wouldn't ever stop dreamin',
Gaming was his hobby,
And went on the wrong lobby,
Then he never stopped leavin'!

Ethan Thorne (11)
Orchard Vale Primary School, Whiddon Valley

Joe Keeble

J oyful
O bservant
E ager

K ind
E lated
E arnest
B arking
L anky
E ffervescent.

Joseph Keeble (11)
Orchard Vale Primary School, Whiddon Valley

I Am

This is who I am.

O livia is...
L oyal
I ndependent
V ibrant
I maginative
A mazing.

Olivia Popps (11)
Orchard Vale Primary School, Whiddon Valley

Me

There was a young lad, name of Thorne,
In 2011, he was born.
He was once very wise,
And won a big prize,
And then, he woke up at dawn.

Oliver Thorne (11)
Orchard Vale Primary School, Whiddon Valley

This Is Me

I was born on the wrong day,
12.12.12 could've been my perfect birthday!
I remember very well that disappointing day,
When my mum said my actual birthday.

When I was one, my dog was always gone,
When I was two, I tried to eat a shoe,
When I was three, I was scared of a bee,
When I was four, I was never a bore,
When I was five, I went to the school hive,
When I was six, I devoured my first Twix,
When I was seven, I wished I was eleven,
When I was eight, I licked a plate,
When I was nine, I tried to drink my mum's wine.

I wish I were the queen bee,
Then everybody would listen to me.
I want to go to Greece or create world peace.

So that's what I am, that's what I will be,
With a T and an E and an M and a P and an I.

So that's what I am, that's what I'll be,
Mr Faz,
Mrs Helen,
Laughing Lao,
Missy me.

A hip, a hop, a hip, hop, hap,
I just gave you the Tempi rap.

Tempi Singhateh
Roecliffe CE Primary School, Roecliffe

This Is Me

Ponies calm me, they never fail,
I brush their silky tail.
Don't forget their beautiful colours,
They are treat smugglers.

Don't forget the two I have,
Star and Toby, they wave a flag.
Esme, my dog, loves their poo,
She also eats my shoe.

Star is old now - 26 in fact,
She puts on a young act.
I always ride, I never stop,
My pony almost pops.

Star shimmers in the light like an actual star,
Riding takes me far.
Every time I get lost in my own world,
My personality gets uncurled.

Toby is only a loan pony,
He likes macaroni.

He likes cuddles and hates puddles,
And doesn't have strong muscles.

Ponies calm me, they never fail,
I brush their silky tail.
Don't forget their beautiful colours,
They are treat smugglers.

Lucy G (9)
Roecliffe CE Primary School, Roecliffe

This Is Me

I was born in 2013,
I remember very well that scary day.

When I was 1, my sister was gone,
When I was 2, I got the big flu,
When I was 3, I made some brown tea,
When I was 4, I started a world war,
When I was 5, I practised the hand jive,
When I was 6, I listened to Harry Styles' new remix,
When I was 7, my nan went to Heaven,
When I was 8, I went on a date,
When I was 9, I chugged some wine.

So that's what I am, that's what I'll be,
With a W, with an I, with an L and an L,
So that's what I am, that's what I'll be,
With a hip, a hop, a hip, hop, hap,
I'm giving you the Will B rap!

William Bennett (8)
Roecliffe CE Primary School, Roecliffe

This Is Me

K ittens are cute and cuddly but they cause catastrophes

I adore stripy zebras too which is why I also want to go to the zoo

T he electric piano transports me to another miraculous world

T errific, tremendous arts and crafts, I could do it all day long

E xclusive dancing with my friends at school, I love to do it because they're all so cool

N arnia is my favourite film but I have many more

S oundlessly as I sleep, I easily dream big!

Isla C (8)

Roecliffe CE Primary School, Roecliffe

This Is Me

I'm who you want to see,
Always thinking twice,
Because I listen to my parents' advice.

I'm a Leeds United dude,
Because they bring the attitude,
They play madly,
Making the other teams play badly.

My favourite animal is the terrifying tiger,
Every time I look, I can see the anger,
It's the king of the jungle,
Ready to rumble.

Most days, I'm a cheerful lad,
Not often you will see me sad,
Like going to school,
Because everyone is cool.

This rapping is fun,
But I have to run.

Milosz Smentek (9)
Roecliffe CE Primary School, Roecliffe

This Is Me

When I was one, I fired a machine gun,
When I was two, I was very brave. I jumped out of
a tree and flew.
When I was three, I saw the sea. It amazed me!
When I was four, I fell on the concrete floor - *ouch!*
When I was five, I did the hand jive,
When I was six, I devoured a sweet mix - delicious!
When I was seven, I walked to Devon,
When I was eight, I went on my first date - like Will!
When I was nine, I hugged a lion - *Roar!*

George R

Roecliffe CE Primary School, Roecliffe

This Is Me

When I was one, I shot 18 mini guns,
When I was two, I destroyed the flu,
When I was three, I voyaged the sea,
When I was four, I destroyed a boar,
When I was five, I destroyed a beehive,
When I was six, I stopped Little Mix,
When I was seven, I destroyed Bleven,
When I was eight, I beat my mate (in a game).

So that's what I am, that's what I'll be,
With an E, with a D,
That's me!

Edward Wright (9)
Roecliffe CE Primary School, Roecliffe

This Is Me Rap

When I was one, I could lift a ton,
When I was two, I ate something blue,
When I was three, I thought I was a bee,
When I was four, I rolled on the floor,
When I was five, I always strived,
When I was six, my house was fixed,
When I was seven, I flew to Heaven,
When I was eight, I dropped a plate,
When I was nine, I was fine,
So this is me,
Isabella - the exciting storyteller.

Isabella Campbell (8)
Roecliffe CE Primary School, Roecliffe

Tiger, My Cat

Tiger is my favourite cat,
What do you think of that?

And I'm here to say,
He's the baddest cat in the UK.

He has lots of fans - can't you see?
Every cat wants to hang with Tiger and me.

He loves food and affection,
Wonder if he could win an election?

I love gardening - and after that,
I can pat and pat,
Who wouldn't want a cat like that?

Georgina L
Roecliffe CE Primary School, Roecliffe

This Is Me

A fabulous football player that always survives the fall,
A marvellous Minecraft survivor but I'm not very tall,
A supreme snake lover, I love all, big and small,
A super sea swimmer but I don't like the fish at all,
An incredible Irish dancer, I could dance all day,
A sonic science explorer, my brain is a storer.

Ida P (9)
Roecliffe CE Primary School, Roecliffe

Fireworks In My Song

B eing me is like a firework exploding
E xcitedness, jumping around like bunnies
N ew songs I try to sing, to join in and be happy
I t is a new way of jumping, laughing and playing
T o join in with others and play with them
A mazing adventures with my friends, sending
things and achieving victory as well

B eing me is something other than music, it is
kindness
A bout helping others, overcoming fights
G reat love for helping but a love for God first
N egative is not in my vocabulary but positive is
A ll who hate me, I love. All who love me, I love
L oving others like my family
L oving haters like my family too.

Benita Bagnall (9)

St Joseph's Catholic Primary School, Deptford

Art Forever, Me Forever

This is me and my art!
Paint, paint, paint, I do it all day,
I love art, it is my priority,
This is me making patterns,
Purple and pink splatters making a creation,
This is me with my bestie having fun, drawing pictures,
Shine bright as your art gets bigger,
This is me being a kid,
Playing on the swing, falling off like a squirrel,
This is me relaxing and chilling,
Having fun looking at my paintings,
This is me trying to be myself,
This is me writing this poem.

Chiamaka Onwochei (9)

St Joseph's Catholic Primary School, Deptford

Proud Of Who I Am

This is me,
Stepping into the spotlight,
Singing my song,
Not doing it wrong.

This is me,
Living my life,
All day, all night,
Doing it right.

This is me,
With my best friends,
Having fun,
Laughing in the sun.

This is me,
An explosion of emotions,
Feeling sad,
Feeling glad.

This is me,
This is me,

Shining all around,
Strong and proud.

Betsy Ebenuwa (8)

St Joseph's Catholic Primary School, Deptford

This Is My Name, Destiny

I look at the clouds, the trees, the bees, but no one sees.

I smell like roses, I use my manners like please.

I shine like a shooting star.

If anyone came up to me, they would feel my skin, Because it's as soft as a pillow.

Every day, I shine bright like a rainbow rising from the sky.

I'm the sun achieving my goals every day.

My face might be brown, but I like, no, I love my colour.

Destiny Onyewachi (9)
St Joseph's Catholic Primary School, Deptford

I Am Nice

I am good at spelling,
I am good at maths,
I am good at science,
I am good at history,
I am good at PE,
I am good at RE,
I am good at topics,
I am good at looking,
I am good at listening,
I am good at hide-and-seek,
I am good at I Spy,
I am good at What's the Time, Mr Wolf?
I am good at learning,
I am good at getting stars,
I am good at drawing.

Enoch Akinsomisoye (9)

St Joseph's Catholic Primary School, Deptford

All About Me

Hi, I am nine and fine,
I shine so bright like a cloud in the sky,
I am shy like a butterfly,
My name is Chantelle,
It means to sing and I love to sing,
It is my time to shine,
Night may come, but I still need my light,
I still need to be bright like a shining star,
Time flies like a shooting star,
It is my time to do what is right,
Soon, I will change what is wrong.

Chantelle Osei (9)
St Joseph's Catholic Primary School, Deptford

I'm Glad To Be Me

I look in the mirror,
And what I do see,
I see the me,
Nobody else can be,
I'm precious,
I'm glad to be me,
My hair,
My face,
My personality,
My size,
My shape,
The colour of my skin,
All make up me,
Outside and in.
Anything I put my mind to,
I know that's what I can do,
No matter what anybody says,
I believe in myself!

Maya Hamdoun (9)
St Joseph's Catholic Primary School, Deptford

All About Me

P atricia is my name and I am 9 years old

A m young and strong, an independent girl

T raining hard to win it all!

R eady to roll, that is I!

I am Patricia, I am 9 years old

C elebrating all, black or white, so come on in before it gets too tight!

I am Patricia, a 9-year-old girl

A nd I hope I win, so fingers crossed!

Patricia Krotka (9)

St Joseph's Catholic Primary School, Deptford

Me, Myself And I

I'm Prince and hobbies are my thing,
My hobbies don't shine,
But my personality is really divine!
I play but don't say I'm lame,
Because if you know,
You will start going with the flow.
Don't ask who I am because
This is me, myself and I,
And I'm divine.
This is my poem
And I will win,
Passing by like a king.

Prince Armah Erzoah (8)
St Joseph's Catholic Primary School, Deptford

Clouds And Me

This is me walking down the street.
With my bright, bold, and beautiful dress.
As the hot sun shines on my skin,
I see myself as a diamond.

I sing a tune and people listen carefully.
As I finish, I see a pool of large gifts.
There is someone sitting on the clouds listening
most attentively.

Elisha Brainard (9)

St Joseph's Catholic Primary School, Deptford

Me And My Life

A danna is my name
D on't be fooled by my height, I am only nine
A few months ago, I was living in Ghana
N ow I'm back in good ol' London
N igeria and Sierra Leone are where I come from
A nd now we've come to the end of my poem.

Adanna Nnani (9)
St Joseph's Catholic Primary School, Deptford

This Is Me

This is me walking to school,
In my bright, bold clothes,
Going to learn about black people,
Who were treated like rubbish,
Singing is my passion,
Having an audience is nice,
Being black is nice,
Life is nice.

Christian Kelly (9)
St Joseph's Catholic Primary School, Deptford

Amazing Me

Brave as a lion, never quiet as a mouse,
Open like a flower and sprouting as I grow,
This is amazing me.

Skilful like a cheetah, intelligent like a cat,
Careful as a snake trying to catch its prey,
Funny as a joker, yet serious if I must,
I want to move forward, past obstacles in my way,
This is amazing me.

I like to play sports but there is always time to
relax,
I like to do exercise but there is always time to
relax,
That's just who I am,
That's just amazing me.

I try my best,
I do my best,
And maybe one day,
I will be the best because,
That's just amazing me.

Angus Campbell (11)
St Mary's RC Primary School, Wimbledon

All About Me

I'm loyal and kind,
I love to be friendly,
I love the colour blue,
And my favourite pet is a cute bunny.

This is me.

I'm mostly happy,
But things can get cloudy,
Just take a deep breath,
And release the anger.

Keep going when things are tough,
Ride the waves when things are rough,
Think of the things you love,
And you'll reach above.

This is me.

I love to play football,
Go out with my friends,
I enjoy acting,
And hope to become an actor one day.

I love having fun,
Or having a run,
Getting together,
And keeping the moment forever.

This is me.

I like to travel around the world,
See each country standing tall,
Visit wonderful places I've been told,
And remember them like a hall of fame.

I'm excited for secondary school,
Even though it's quite scary,
Just follow the rules and enjoy,
As it will go quickly.

This is me!

I hope you enjoyed my poem,
How it's okay to be yourself,
Just be you,
And you'll be fine,

This is me!

Troy Edwards (11)
St Mary's RC Primary School, Wimbledon

This Is Me

In the winter, I like to play in the snow,
In the winter, I wear fuzzy gloves and a warm,
fluffy coat,
In the winter, I drink hot soup and eat warm ravioli,
In the winter, I want to go ice skating but the cold
is unbearable.
This is me!

In autumn, I like to make big leaf piles with my
friends,
In autumn, I wear cosy turtlenecks, leggings and
fluffy boots,
In autumn, I collect leaves and turn them into art,
In autumn, I want to get a pool of leaves and jump
in it but that isn't necessary.
This is me!

In spring, I like to watch the flowers bloom,
In spring, I wear long-sleeved shirts and jeans,
In spring, I spend my days watching the plants
bloom,
In spring, I want to go outside but it is a bit cold.
This is me!

In the summer, I like to collect different types of flowers,
In the summer, I wear short-sleeved shirts and skirts,
In the summer, I go to warm sunny beaches,
In the summer, I want to make a thousand daisy chains but it's too tiring.
This is me!

Julia Ornowska (11)
St Mary's RC Primary School, Wimbledon

My Emotion Jar

There's a special jar I keep somewhere,
Tucked deep away,
Filled with colours; green, blue and red,
This is my emotion jar.

First, there's happy,
With its glossy orange coat,
Showing off its marshmallow teeth,
It's always ready to give you a hug,
When sad has got you tangled up.

Talking about sad,
He's always moping about,
Feeling sorry for himself,
He only complains when he speaks
Especially when the others are near.

At least there's calm to restore the peace,
He knows how to stop the fuss,
With an Om and a namaste,
Everything is alright,
Until someone starts it up again.

It's probably mischievous,
Who makes you laugh or cry,
Maybe with a whoopee cushion,
Or paper and string,
He's a master at his thing.

So that's my emotion jar,
And the colourful things in it,
And though they're not all perfect,
I cherish each one inside.

Francesca Brooks (10)
St Mary's RC Primary School, Wimbledon

This Is Me!

Creative like a dolphin
Dancing through the waves

Observant like a bear
Which lingers in its cave

Crafty like a spider
That spins her web gracefully

Loyal like a golden retriever
Guarding its home courageously

Magnificent like a caterpillar
Full of surprises

Beautiful like a butterfly
That falls and rises

Calm like a tortoise
Patiently taking his time

Fast like a cheetah
Racing to the finish line

Small like a mouse
That cowers away

Mighty like an elephant
That protects you all the way

Wise like an owl
Watching in the night

Passionate like a bee
Buzzing in the daylight

Shy like an antelope
Hiding in the trees

Brave like a lion
Who's not scared of what he sees

THIS IS ME!

Adriana Ramos (11)
St Mary's RC Primary School, Wimbledon

About Myself

I am going to tell you about myself,
I am a funny, warm-hearted person,
I love being artistic,
And I love painting,
I love to talk,
Or do comprehension,
I look like this:
I am mixed-race,
I have black eyes,
And black hair,
And that is me.

I am going to tell you about my teachers,
Their names are Miss Donaghy and Miss Murray
John,
They always help me to improve my work,
To help me be the best that I can be,
To help me before I go to secondary,
Be a better person in general,
They are both also very funny,
And have a great sense of humour,
And that is enough about them.

I am now going to tell you about my best friend,
She is called Amelia Kelly,
She is always there for me,
She is always ready for anything,
She is the best,
Going to secondary,
That is enough about her.

Gabriella Wilson (10)

St Mary's RC Primary School, Wimbledon

All About Me

Woke up in the morning on a lovely day,
Wishing everyone a very happy day,
Everyone's not perfect, I sang to myself,
Don't listen to others but me and yourself.

On Tuesday, I woke up a little bit sad,
My mother came up and that made me glad,
She told me to sing to the sun,
And that helped me, so my poem goes on.

On Wednesday, it came to my mind,
To write a poem about my own life,
I went downstairs to start my plan,
It started great, so I carried on.

Thursday came, it was a brand-new day,
I discovered myself wanting to be an artist one
day,
It's my hidden talent,
No opinions to delay.

Friday at last,
I can now have a rest,

Maybe play some Roblox or do some art, I guess,
My brother comes in and annoys me again,
As I start an eruption, he flees from me again.

Hailey Chan (11)
St Mary's RC Primary School, Wimbledon

This Is Me...

I may be happy,
I may be sad,
I may be quiet,
I may be loud,
I may be good,
I may be bad,
But overall...
This is me!

My eyes may be blue,
My eyes may be brown,
My hair may be black,
As dark as the ground,
My hair might be blonde,
My hair may be brown,
But overall...
This is me!

I may like art,
I may like maths,
I may like English,
But you may not like that,

But overall...
This is me!

The N is for nice,
The I is for intelligent,
The K is for kind,
The O is for open-hearted
The L is for loving,
I may be other things,
But overall...
This is me!

Nikol Pilichowska (11)
St Mary's RC Primary School, Wimbledon

This Is Me

I am...

Intelligent like a dolphin,
That dives into the sea.

Busy like a bee,
That buzzes to schools.

Brave like a lion,
Never quiet like a mouse.

Open like a flower,
That makes the seeds grow.

Fast like a cheetah,
That always gets there on time.

And creative like an owl,
That flies in the night sky.

Kind like a bunny,
That hops itself to bed.

Clean like a whale,
That swims for its health.

Understanding like a snake,
That slithers its way through arguments.

Skilful like a meerkat,
Intelligent like a cat.

Careful like a tiger,
Trying to catch its prey.

And smart like a chimpanzee,
That swings itself through trees.

And that is me.

Amelia Ciecka (11)
St Mary's RC Primary School, Wimbledon

Me

Me,
A unique human being,
There is no one like me in this wide universe.

Happy me,
Now this is the key,
Happy me laughs,
Full of energy, she climbs and reads,
She sips her milky Eko,
With a sneaky pinch of sugar gladly.
This is happy me.

But calm me is a different me,
She sits at the top of a tree,
Observing the world below her,
She pats Leo, stroking his soft fur,
Or plays a tune on the piano,
Everything else is a blur,
This is calm me.

Now tired me,
Tired me is a bored me,
She sighs and taps her shoe,

She stares into space with a blank mind,
But don't worry, she's still kind,
This is tired me.

Me,
Not always perfect,
But I love her all the same; I try.
This is me.
Who are you?

Ellie Narainsamy Mouriz (11)
St Mary's RC Primary School, Wimbledon

This Is Me

This is me,
When I look into the distance and see the sun,
Due to that, I know the day will be fun.
My dog gives me cuddles,
Later on, I will wash him in the bubbles.
When my life gets tough,
My heart goes rough,
So then I play with my most calming stuff.
At the end of the day,
I look at the sunset,
And never regret what I did that day.

This is me,
When we go to the safari park,
We always stay till it gets dark.
The jaguars, lions and leopards,
They all love to eat,
Their prepared luxurious meat.
The lion's mane is as smooth as rain.
When I do my art,
I doodle at the start of the safari park,
Whilst the bark is eaten by the giraffe.

This is me,
When I lay down my head in bed,
I remember what I said,
This is me.

Elano Jorge (11)
St Mary's RC Primary School, Wimbledon

This Is Me

Purple is my colour,
It looked like the galaxy,
Such a beautiful sight,
When my eyes look away,
A blank blue sky has awoken.
This is me.

I love hedgehogs, so cute and neat,
They eat berries that are so sweet,
They have prickly backs that can shock,
But it won't stop me from loving them a lot.
This is me.

Tennis is my sport,
Even though I'm short,
I reach the ball every time,
With the racket in my hands,
And that's when I shine.
This is me.

There is a game I like,
It's called Roblox,
It's very fun to play,

Especially on weekdays.
This is me.

And now you know,
All about me,
As you can see, I'm very unique,
To everyone around me.
This is me!

Hugo Barra (11)
St Mary's RC Primary School, Wimbledon

This Is Me!

This is me,
This is me,
I like to be free,
Go outside on tons of walks,
And see all of the amazing wonderful sites,
Meet new people every day,
Always say, "Come on, let's go play."

Sometimes I am lazy,
Sometimes I am bad,
But that will never change who I truly really am,
People think I'm kind, especially my best friends,
Oh, something very special that I really have to tell
you,
Be yourself and don't act like anybody else.

I love to be fun,
I am also very crazy,
It's kinda my speciality,
Like an emoji face, I may be funny,
Like a rainbow cake, I may be happy,
With sprinkles on top, I may be jolly,

But let me tell you something,
This is me and nobody can change me.

Georgia Kelly (11)
St Mary's RC Primary School, Wimbledon

This Is Me!

Red:
Red is when I'm angry,
When I get all rude inside,
I want to scream and shout,
And throw my thoughts aside.

I snuggle up to my dog,
Take a few deep breaths,
Talk to my mum and dad,
And give myself a rest.

Yellow:
Yellow is when I'm nervous,
Before something new,
My palms start to sweat,
And I start to tap my shoe.

I remember I am fine,
And start to read my book,
Quickly turned the pages,
Just before I shook.

Green:
Green is when I'm calm,
When my heart is full of peace,
My heart feels like a cloud,
As soft as a sheep's fleece.

I love to sing and dance,
And wear a banana smile,
Spread all of my happiness,
For at least a mile.

Helen Golus (11)
St Mary's RC Primary School, Wimbledon

Who Is She?

Hello,
I am she!
And this is my nationality,
She is American and Indian,
And does not like tea.
She likes to be amazing, energetic and friendly,
But most importantly,
That is she!

She doesn't like dresses, skirts or dirt,
Okay, maybe she doesn't mind dirt,
But she likes to be free,
Like a bee,
Flying near the sea,
That is she!

To be like she,
You must be,
Awesome, fit, fast,
Never be last,
Funny and fantastic,

Like that bee,
That is she!

But wait!
You can't be like me,
You are your own you,
I am my own she,
Iliana is she, and that she is me!
And let me tell you that,
This is me!

Iliana Turbin (11)
St Mary's RC Primary School, Wimbledon

This Is Me

My friends, my family, my peers,
My ballet, my sport, my hobbies,
This is me!

My passion for everything I do,
My imagination is out of this world!
This is me!

My candle that burns brighter every day,
My blanket that covers me in kindness,
This is me!

The opportunities that I have,
The chances that I have been given,
This is me!

My creativity that sparks like a firework,
My friendship that reaches out like a hand,
This is me!

My ideas that burst out like thunder,
And my eagerness to learn more,
This is me!

Isabel Bonney (11)
St Mary's RC Primary School, Wimbledon

This Is Me!

This is me, a girl in a tree,
Friends, cuddles and bubbles are all about me,
Sitting in the morning breeze, drinking a cup of tea,
This is all me.
Having fun in Pizza Hut,
Riding horses during Sunday lunch,
Then taking a little munch,
Food is all me,
Helping an elder cross the road,
Studying in my lovely school,
Dreaming on a pretty cloud,
This is me!

Like the colour green,
I run into the tree,
Definitely not moaning,
As I sprint while eating mint,
What a lovely day it was,
Oh, now it's dusk,
Wish I must,
This is me!

Sophii Skrzynska (11)
St Mary's RC Primary School, Wimbledon

141

All About Me

Butterflies fly and my friendship grows,
When I sing,
I wish to be on a stag,
I love my family, especially my twin,
My best friend is kind and loyal too,
Her name is Gabriella and she is great too.

I got braces on the 13th October,
They are ever so annoying,
But they do their job well.
I love to be brave,
I love to be kind,
I am tough and I love butterflies.

I am a twin,
My sis is amazing,
She is a delight to see every day,
Georgia Kelly is her name,
My teacher, Miss Donaghy, is amazing,
This is me,
Amelia Kelly.

Amelia Kelly (11)
St Mary's RC Primary School, Wimbledon

This Is Me!

This is me, a ray of sunlight,
This is me, a rhyming tune,
This is me, a bird singing in the sky,
And an angel hovering up high.

This is me, a smart, intelligent mind,
This is me, a person full of laughter,
This is me, an overthinker,
A worrier with a barrier of love.

This is me, a dancing spirit with a black or white
robe,
This is me, a girl living in a house of four, in a calm
and peaceful street,
This is me, an open mystery book waiting to be
read,
This is me, the whole alphabet with a variety of
hobbies.

This is me!

Carolina Pontes Fernandes (11)

St Mary's RC Primary School, Wimbledon

Leo's Wishes

Leo is my name,
I have a great life and all,
But still no fame,
What a shame!

I wish I could be a football star,
And have my face on a chocolate bar,
I wish I could go far,
In my fancy sports car.

I like hosting my friends,
And also a bit of boasting about myself,
I do not take it as shame,
I take it as fame.

I wish I could feast like a king,
And have ownership of an amazing thing,
Only time will tell,
Will this future ring on my bell?

Leo is my name,
Will I have fame,
Or shame?

Leo Farag (11)
St Mary's RC Primary School, Wimbledon

144

This Is Me!

This is me,
Always trying hard,
Being resilient and caring,
Lots of hard moments in my life,
Needing to leave everything behind,
With no date to come back,
Moments of happiness come and go,
This is me.

Suddenly, the day to go back comes,
My heart breaks,
I feel cheerfulness,
And I feel depression,
I don't know what to feel,
I don't know what to think,
This is me.

But even in the hardest moments,
The happiness returns to your mind,
The sun will always come out,
This is me.

Martina Cardenas (11)
St Mary's RC Primary School, Wimbledon

Truly Me

I am a cloud,
Heavy with dread,
Light with joy,
Calm when in bed.

I am a candle,
Flickering when I'm sad,
Blazing when I'm angry,
Shining when I'm glad.

I am a flower,
Happiness is my light,
Sadness is my rain,
I need them to thrive.

I am a book,
I can be adventurous,
I can be entertaining,
I can be mysterious.

I am a spark,
That lights up the dark,
I am a flame,

I hide with shame,
I may be bad, I may be good,
But this is all truly me.

Alexandra El Khoury (11)

St Mary's RC Primary School, Wimbledon

My Deep Mind

I work all day and night,
Silently and out of sight,
Some say I am bright and kind,
However, I am just a mind,

Whenever I sleep,
My daily dreams come to reality,
I enter a zone beyond familiarity,
A place with no maximum capacity,

During the day,
I work away like the M25,
Making sure that my owner stays alive,
Thoughts fly by at the speed of light,

Overall,
I work extremely hard,
To make my owner move, speak and sleep at night,
I am not always right,
But I am just a mind.

Marko Dobrovolskyi (11)
St Mary's RC Primary School, Wimbledon

I, Aiden

When I am ignored and alone, anger strikes me,
I turn red-hot if I forget to breathe.
Steam blows out of my ears when I am told to go to my room,
Or when I am told to use a broom.

I sweat, I shake and tears pour out of my eyes,
This happens when I tell lies.
I wasn't built for guilt,
As it makes my heart tilt.

Gyozas and pizzas are what make me jump,
And what helps me avoid the bumps
In the path, towards my last breath on the road ahead,
And what keeps me from my bed.

Aiden Farrugia (11)
St Mary's RC Primary School, Wimbledon

My Name Is Aëlis

My name is Aëlis,
I love an adventure.

When I feel sad,
I do a cartwheel.
When I am nervous,
I listen to music.
When I am angry,
I read a good book.
When I am frustrated,
I climb a tree.

My name is Aëlis,
I love an adventure.

I care for others,
I care about nature.
I love the sea,
And I love animals.
When everything is at peace,
I feel so zen.
I'm not perfect,
But I do try.

My name is Aëlis,
I love an adventure.

Aëlis Joalland (11)
St Mary's RC Primary School, Wimbledon

All About Me

I am an average girl,
With an average life and average dreams.
I want to be an actress,
Who stars in many plays,
Disney movies, Netflix shows,
Maybe even Broadway!
My classmates say I can sing,
Unique and optimistic.
I feel gifted when it comes to theatre,
Like it's where I belong.
When I sing, I feel so free,
Like the rhythm is controlling me!
I want to dance until the dawn,
And twirl my heart out forever more!
Maybe I am not so average after all.

Georgia Bate (11)
St Mary's RC Primary School, Wimbledon

This Is Me

I have blonde hair, green eyes,
I am who I want to be,
Born in 2011,
This is me.

I am tall, kind, smart,
I can speak three languages,
I like to play the lead part,
This is me.

My hobbies are gymnastics and swimming,
My favourite subject in school is PE,
I like winning,
This is me.

I'm a girl with one sibling,
A mum, a dad,
I don't care if you don't like me,
Just don't be mad,
'Cause this is me.

Grace Castelli (10)
St Mary's RC Primary School, Wimbledon

I, Amelia Maria Nyack

I, Amelia Maria Nyack,
I am kind when touched,
And mean when punched.

I've overcome what's bad,
And hated what's sad.

I like being on the beach,
With the sand in-between my toes,
And the sun hitting my face,
Gives me a smile of Grace.

A dventurous
M indful
E cstatic
L oving
I ndependent
A mazing!

I'm happy that I have a loving family,
And amazing friends.

Amelia Maria Nyack (11)
St Mary's RC Primary School, Wimbledon

This Is Me

A normal girl,
Now that is me,
Curly hair,
Luscious lips,
Talented,
And sufficient,
As you can see,
Just a girl,
A normal one,
That is brave,
And mischievous,
You've guessed it,
Now that is me,
Just a young Portuguese girl,
Kind-hearted,
And friendly,
That's me.
I have three siblings,
All very cheeky,
It's Rita, Thomas,
Mariana and me!

Madalena Orvalho (11)
St Mary's RC Primary School, Wimbledon

What Should I Be?

What should I be? What should I be?
Maybe a sailor sailing over the sea,
Or a veterinarian living as a vet,
And caring for every pet,
An astronaut flying into space,
A racer picking up her pace,
Maybe a chef making amazing food,
Or a teacher in a mood,
A police officer catching bad guys,
An exterminator killing lots of flies,
What should I be? What should I be?
I know - me,
Just me.

Tabitha Keefe (8)
St Mary's RC Primary School, Wimbledon

This Is Me

I am kind, caring, loyal,
I love sports like football, racing and biking,
I have blonde hair,
My favourite animals are dogs,
My favourite YouTubers inspired me
To become a YouTube creator.

My favourite food is pesto ravioli,
My favourite book to read is Diary of a Wimpy Kid,
My dream is to become a YouTuber or a footballer,
I am happy when I do things that I like.
This is me!

Lukasz Zelazowski (11)
St Mary's RC Primary School, Wimbledon

Dream Time

Bedtime,
Cosy like a caring, cuddly cat,
I close my eyes,
Drifting, drifting, drifting
Away...
To dream time.
My eyes glitter in the moonlight,
I am a dancing queen on the stage,
My black dress sparkles with shimmering stars,
Suddenly, I trip,
Falling, falling, falling,
I open my eyes,
Dream time has disappeared,
Rise and shine time.

Georgie Brooks (9)
St Mary's RC Primary School, Wimbledon

How To Make Me

To make me, you need:
The glow of an owl's eyes at night,
The sparkle of a grain of glistening glitter,
For my eyes.

To make me, you need:
The body of a deer coated with blue paint,
Followed by the smell of strawberries,
For my body.

To make me, you need:
The panic of a snail being baked,
The dancing of a tree for my emotions.

Maya Sputo (8)
St Mary's RC Primary School, Wimbledon

I Am Me

I'm a kind, creative girl,
I help out with everything.

H is for helpful with all the things I do
E is for energetic, jumping like a monkey in a zoo
L is for loyal, you can trust me
E is for elegant, I'm very pretty
N is for nice as I like rice
A is for acrobatic as I'm quite energetic.

Helena Bourbon (9)

St Mary's RC Primary School, Wimbledon

This Is Me

My dancing, my art,
My smiling face.

My happiness, my kindness,
My endless chase.

My netball, my swimming,
My slow pace.

My sister, my parents,
My favourite place.

My pizza, my chocolate cake,
My strawberry lace.

My high school, my basketball,
My trip to space.

This is me.

Arianna Vallejo de Lange (11)
St Mary's RC Primary School, Wimbledon

Laura

A dash of love,
This is me.

A sprinkle of amazing,
This is me.

A blob of unique,
This is me.

A mix of relaxation,
This is me.

A hint of astonishing,
This is me.

Bake in the oven,
And out comes Laura.

This is what makes me!

Laura Scripps (11)
St Mary's RC Primary School, Wimbledon

Being In My World!

It is me with a great golden heart,
Superstar, it's me,
Only me and who I am,
Absolutely amazing Capucine,
A horse lover,
With hope and blessings,
From Heaven above,
Looking forward
To catch my dream,
To win my race,
Just like me,
Being in my world!

Capucine Tanqueray (11)
St Mary's RC Primary School, Wimbledon

This Is Me

This is me,
This is me, born in 2011,
Smart, sporty kid,
Brown hair, brown eyes,
This is me!

This is me,
Loves football,
Kind, caring friend,
Dream of becoming
The greatest footballer
In history,
I have a big family,
This is me!

Stefano La Rosa (11)

St Mary's RC Primary School, Wimbledon

Amazing Me

My name is Thomas and I'm 11,
When I was 7, I started to like football,
When I'm happy, I'm a rainbow,
When I'm angry, I'm thunder,
I'm from Portugal.
Blue skies, nice beaches,
Water as clear as a glass bottle.

Thomas Cruz (11)
St Mary's RC Primary School, Wimbledon

Until...

Year 6 has come,
SATs have passed,
Our play is here,
Auditions have flown,
I am here writing,
My story has stopped,
Next time I write,
There will be a lot,
Until...

Noah Simpson (11)
St Mary's RC Primary School, Wimbledon

Here Is Me

My name is Mia, I'm 10 years old,
I love to do activities and I think I'm quite bold.
I sometimes get scared of heights and nights,
So I bite my nails to take away the fright.
My dream job is to be an engineer,
Electronic or bionic, I have no idea.
When I get older, I'll make a decision,
But either way, it's going to take a lot of revision.
But for now, I'm going to enjoy being ten,
Messing and playing around with my friends.

Mia Wallis-Figa (10)
Sundridge & Brasted CE (VC) Primary School, Sundridge

A Day In The Life Of Charlie

On a fresh, frosty field, football fever is found,
Not forgetting how I like hunting with the hounds.

As I score from the halfway line,
My football career is about to shine.
The cheer from the crowd,
Represents my family being proud.

As I ride my motorbike through the muddy tracks,
There's no other feeling like when we go roaring back.
And when it's time to rest and be calm,
I like to find myself chilling on the farm.

Charlie Hawley (11)
Sundridge & Brasted CE (VC) Primary School, Sundridge

This Is Me, Nate

Sometimes I'm happy, sometimes I'm sad,
And every so often, I'm a little bit bad.

I try to be me, but I want to fit in,
How can I do that when I think differently?

I'm loud when I should be quiet,
I laugh when I should not,
I'm silly when it's serious,
But how can I not?

My escape is my gaming - I shut everything out,
It's quiet and peaceful and helps me out.

Nate De Bono (11)
Sundridge & Brasted CE (VC) Primary School, Sundridge

Amelia

A is for adorable

M is for messy

E is for excitable

L is for loyal

I is for impatient

A is for angelic.

Amelia Newlands (9)
Sundridge & Brasted CE (VC) Primary School, Sundridge

I Am Willow

I am Willow and Willow is me,
I like to play and eat all day,
So hop on your feet and feel the beat.

Willow Sawkins (9)

Sundridge & Brasted CE (VC) Primary School, Sundridge

This Is Me

T his is me, as happy as can be
H ear the wonders about me and my family
I like to play sports and in tennis, the ball looks
like lightning as it flies through the air
S ometimes I cycle to Richmond Park and feel
relaxed and happy when I have done it

I love sport, cycling, climbing, cooking and
gardening
S miling as I go

M y personality is unique and I am different
E ager to explore the outer world.

Ram Bhalla Singh (9)
Willington Prep School, Wimbledon

The Boy And The Dragon

Once in a faraway land,
Life was in the dragon's hand.
The dragon had crushed all far and near,
Everything except a little pier.
On that pier, stood a minuscule guild,
Just preparing for their ultimate build.
And once in a moment of joy,
One lady just gave birth to a boy!
This boy was instructed to kill the dragon,
And that's what he did in a wagon!

That boy is James.

James Douglas (8)

Willington Prep School, Wimbledon

Sports

There once was a man who lived in a fort.
Who all day long he dreamt of nothing but sport...
Hockey, football, rugby and cricket.
He dreamt of them all but not hitting the wicket.
He dreamt of one day becoming a world-class athlete.
But it turned out that he was the perfect type of mathlete.
What a shame for a man who lives in a fort,
Who all day long dreams of nothing but sport...

Perry Davis (8)
Willington Prep School, Wimbledon

I Am Who I Am

I am not the smartest but I try my hardest

A crostic poems I find easy
M assages are what I like

W illington is where I fit!
H ow kind and caring, I am
O utrageously good at computing

I love doughnuts

A rms full of love
M erry all day long.

Kieran Bourne (10)
Willington Prep School, Wimbledon

Me, Myself And Chocolate

N ever did I think I could be so happy

A s I bite into my sumptuous and mouth-watering chocolate

T his I thought was a stairway to Heaven

H ave I ever tasted something more delicious?

A s the chocolate melts in my mouth

N ow I regret how much I have eaten.

Nathan Whooley (8)

Willington Prep School, Wimbledon

Me

W ith a love of animals and sports

I am me

L ight brown hair and eyes as blue as the sky

L ook at me

I nterested in football, cricket and swimming

A lways me

M y life, my time, this is me!

William Booth (10)

Willington Prep School, Wimbledon

Bat Watching

Fluttering, flittering, fleeting, skittering,
The bats burst out like a cloud of ash.

Swerving, zipping, instinctively flipping,
The evening acrobats dash.

Deftly dancing, artfully darting,
Whirring wings above me flash.

Flickering, twisting, skittishly skimming,
My heart leaps at their needle squeak.

Zigzagging, twirling, swiftly swerving,
Detector splutters as they streak.

Weaving, whirling, agilely turning,
Bats seem wondrous to me.

Kenzie Lowe (11)
Woodbridge Park Education Service, Isleworth

YoungWriters Est. 1991

YOUNG WRITERS INFORMATION

We hope you have enjoyed reading this book – and that you will continue to in the coming years.

If you're the parent or family member of an enthusiastic poet or story writer, do visit our website **www.youngwriters.co.uk/subscribe** and sign up to receive news, competitions, writing challenges and tips, activities and much, much more! There's lots to keep budding writers motivated!

If you would like to order further copies of this book, or any of our other titles, then please give us a call or order via your online account.

Young Writers
Remus House
Coltsfoot Drive
Peterborough
PE2 9BF
(01733) 890066
info@youngwriters.co.uk

Join in the conversation!
Tips, news, giveaways and much more!

f YoungWritersUK **Y** YoungWritersCW **@** youngwriterscw